Chad's Playbook
to
Effective Fathering

Copyright © 2014 Chad D. Bumgarner
All rights reserved
ISBN: 1937118525
ISBN: 978-1937118525

INTRODUCTION

I never would have guessed in a million years that a book like this was inside of me. I remember months ago meeting a good friend of mine at a book store on a rainy Saturday afternoon. We were introduced through his twin brother who I went to college with. We shared a common interest and wanted to meet to see if we could somehow collaborate on something in the future. That meeting turned out to be the start of a major movement that's about to take place. We spoke at length about the types of leadership that needs to be in place in our neighborhoods and communities as well as government. We also discussed the importance of our young and adult men who are lost and need some type of support, education and guidance.

This was the day that my dear friend, Denard Ash, shared his vision with me. He was able to see a need for these men in the form of a men's conference which was structured around educating the "complete man". He went on to explain his vision and how, in the conference, it would be an uplifting and encouraging experience while educating them on finance, politics, health, relationships, spirituality and fatherhood. He knew that the men out there could be helped.......they just needed someone to show them the way and empower them. As we continued to discuss the conference, I could feel that this was not going to be just some run of the mill conference. This one would change lives and enlighten minds.

We started to breakdown what exactly he wanted to cover in the conference and one thing he mentioned was fatherhood. We spoke at length about how important it is to have a father or positive male figure in every child's life. He then asked me about my kids and my relationship with them. As I began to speak, he just stared at me while I went on about my kids and how much time I spend with them and so on. He stopped me after a while and asked me if I would speak at the conference about fatherhood. I said, "huh"? It threw me for a loop. I was expecting him to eventually ask me to speak on a certain aspect of leadership. He followed up by saying that he really felt my passion when I spoke about my children and that other fathers out there need to know what I know about the importance of a relationship with our children.

Needless to say I was hesitant, but eventually I accepted the task. That's when it gets better. He then asks me to write a book about fatherhood for the conference. He said, "Chad, men are going to be there and they are going to need what you are talking about." It took a while to set in because I didn't agree with him at the time. The beautiful thing about it is...............God always knows whose path you should cross in order to get His work done! I fought this thing with Denard for a while. I just didn't see the need to write a book about fatherhood when there are literally thousands of book already in existence. He told me that those books don't have my passion and my way with words. I tell you the truth..........he stayed on me and stayed on me until I finally accepted the challenge and completed it. God is so good! He knows what's inside of you even when you don't! He knew how to get it out and He knew who to use to do it.

This book is written with love and hopefully some insight for men who don't have a relationship with their child(ren) or have a strained relationship. It comes from a couple of viewpoints..........mine as a father and also from the viewpoint of the child in the situation where their father isn't around. Now I was blessed to have my father and mother in my life and I still do to this day. However, everyone doesn't have that same background but it still doesn't change the fact that children need their fathers in their lives. I wrote this book to light a fire within fathers so that they will want to build a relationship with their child and create some long lasting memories and incorporate life lessons, values and morals that their child(ren) will need in order to face whatever life brings them.

DEDICATION

I would like to dedicate this book to my nephew, Charlie Lee. I thank you for allowing me to come into your life and become the father figure you weren't able to have. I really enjoyed watching you grow up into the fine young man that you are. I do understand that we've had our share of ups and downs and differences but you always listened and took heed to my advice. I love the fact that you are mentoring a young man now and that you are guiding him much the same way as I did you.

I wish you nothing but the best and much success in your life. May the good Lord continue to smile upon you and grant you favor, grace, peace and love all the days of your life.

Thank you Denard, for believing I could do this thru Him.

To my father, Lee Bumgarner……thank you for raising me the way that you did. I love you unconditionally. Thank you for being my hero!!

CONTENTS

Introduction..................................Pg.5

Dedication....................................Pg.9

Whoa! I'm gonna be a dad!............Pg.13

Present VS. Available.....................Pg.21

A Present Father............................Pg.27

Fathers and Sons............................Pg.35

Fathers and Daughters...................Pg.43

Excuses are for the weak!...............Pg.51

Your seed = A nation!....................Pg.57

Be relatable!..................................Pg.63

Don't Disappoint!..........................Pg.67

Conclusion....................................Pg.73

WHOA!! I'M GONNA BE A DAD!

It was a late chilly night on March 3rd when my first child was born. I'll never forget that feeling when she and I met for the very first time, face to face. She was still in the doctor's hands with her eyes closed and silent. The doctor struggled somewhat to retrieve her because it seemed as though she didn't want to come out. Due to prior complications with my wife's contractions, the doctor saw fit to have an emergency caesarian. They cleared out her mouth and nasal passages and gave her a nice little swat on the bottom……..and she started crying.

I'm in love!

It was at that moment when I couldn't believe that I could love someone so much that I would do anything for. Even die for without any hesitation. The nurses cleaned her up, measured her, gave her a few shots, cleaned out her eyes, etc. and then asked me if I would like to hold her.

"Yes, I would" I said.

As I held my baby girl for the first time I knew in my heart that I was going to do whatever it took to keep her protected, healthy, warm, comfortable and happy (the latter is quite difficult as the years go by!). She looked me in my eyes for the first time and my heart just melted. She had me wrapped around her little finger already. I proceeded to take her to my wife so that she could see her. My wife gently spoke to her, "hey baby"! She immediately looked right into my wife's eyes as if she wanted to say, "Hey, I know that voice!"

After spending some time with mommy in the emergency room, we (baby girl and I) jetted off to the baby nursery where they really clean up the baby and put a diaper on her and a monitor. I told my wife that I would reunite back with her in her room later. I never left my daughter's side during her first 48 hours in this world. I was determined to be the dad that kids dreamed of. Then it hit me…………..how could a man not want to be a part of his child's life? How could he allow ANYTHING to come between him and his relationship with his seed, regardless of the status between him and the mother?

I didn't dwell on that for too long because I was in a different situation and I had planned on keeping it that way. My situation is that, I was and still am, in love with the mother of my daughters. We've been married for 14 years now and she and I plan to keep it that way.

Now, this is not to say that your path has to be exactly like mine, but what I am saying is, if you don't have a relationship with your child or children, you should keep reading. Every generation has a plethora of children that grow up without a dad or father figure in the home and I don't care what anyone says, it DOES affect them. There's a reason God makes the child from a man AND a woman. Children need that male guidance and discipline and structure and most importantly that VALIDATION from their fathers. Don't get me wrong, there are a lot of single moms out there that are really doing a bang up job. But you can't tell me that having that man around (a good, responsible man) the home sure wouldn't be nice, especially while raising children.

For so long single mothers have had to be strong and play the role that they were not designed to play. A child is supposed to have BALANCE in their lives so that they understand how one compliments the other (ie; the woman compliments the man or vice versa). Fathers are to be leaders for their children. The very first lesson of leadership should be taught by the fathers. It is our nature to love, protect and lead but we do these things in our own way which, a lot of times, hurt the ones we love. Whatever the situation is with the mother it should not, must not, cannot, negatively impact or deny you the opportunity and the honor of establishing a relationship with and raising your child.

Being a father can be a very scary thing because children don't come with instruction manuals. On the flip side, that's the beauty of it! Think about it, this gives you the opportunity to actually get to KNOW your child. What I'm saying is, now you have to really pay attention to patterns, actions and the various cries and what they mean. Stop thinking and believing that it's the woman's job to figure all of that out! You are the man……..act like it! We, as men, fall into this absurd thinking that certain things dealing with children (if not all) are supposed to be the woman's job. If you care to do some reflection on when you were a kid (and didn't have your father), how many times did something happen to you and you really just wanted your dad around to listen or kiss your "owie" or put an arm around you and say, "it's gonna be alright lil' man, daddy's got you." Instead, momma has to play her role and your father's role as best she can. No disrespect to the moms out there but sometimes it's only a dad's comfort that can sooth a child's issue.

Men have this preconception of what they should and shouldn't be doing with a child from infancy all the way up until college or beyond. It's really sad and it's also the reason why there are a ton of people out there in the world today that have never really gotten over a lot of issues pertaining to their father not being around. Men, we are so crucial to our children's lives it's utterly ridiculous. Where there is a lack of men or male figures in the home there is instability of some sort. The child is off balance and for a while they don't seem to understand why.

I get it. Being a dad for the first time is scary but it can also be a defining moment in your life as well when you decide to be there for your child no matter what. Think about growing a flower. You plant the seed (that's the easy part!) then you water it daily and make sure it gets enough sunlight. You continue to care for the seed until it becomes a flower. It's funny, men will nurture their careers. They will nurture their hobbies. However, when it comes to their very own child or children, there are more excuses than you can throw a rock at. Could you imagine allowing someone you help to create go through life without a dad around to make them feel safe and protected from harm's way. Even women look for that trait in a man when dating or trying to decide if a particular man is the right man for her. All women want to be with a man with whom they feel safe. By you making a commitment and being there for your child, you could eliminate the years of hurt, disappointment, anger and bitterness your child would have had towards you. You have the ability to help your child not to become just another statistic. It's time to put away your selfishness and man up to embrace your responsibility as a father and as a man.

I cannot stress enough how important fathers are in their children's lives. This lack of visibility and participation is deteriorating our society at an alarming rate. I was reading an article a while back on *www.lifesitenews.com* and it was talking about how several studies show that the fatherless children here have a major negative impact on our society. It goes on to illustrate that absent fathers were linked to higher rates of negative juvenile activities. On the other hand, children that have fathers in their lives early in their childhood have fewer behavioral problems and higher intellectual abilities as they grow older. Children without their fathers are highly likely to grow up in poverty. Children in a two-parent household will enjoy an average income of about $80,000.00 while a single mom will have an average of about $24,000.00.

What I have just given you are statistics from this particular website based off of numerous studies that they have performed (here in the U.S. and in Canada). I'm not telling you that you should get married because if you don't have any connection with the mother then you just don't. What I am saying is that the child that the two of you had together deserves more. They deserve your love, protection and a commitment that you will do whatever you need to in order to be present and available in their lives and establish a relationship that the both of you will treasure for an entire lifetime. Men, we are the cornerstone of society and raising our children ensures our legacy on this planet.

QUICK FATHER TIPS

- The most important thing about being a father is "being there" for your child.
- Don't allow your child to be a statistic ......give them what they deserve....a father
- Don't allow your relationship with the mother to hinder your relationship with the child. Find a way to make it work.
- This is THE MOST IMPORTANT ROLE you will ever have in life.…..make it count.

Present Vs. Available

Let's be totally honest and fair here……..you have quite a bit of children out there who do have fathers in their lives and the children are still lack balance. Honestly, that's just as bad as not being there ….. it's even worse. There's a story I remember reading either on Facebook or from an email and it was actually in cartoon form. It showed a young son eagerly trying to gain the attention of his dad so that he could ask him a question. The dad would gently brush his son aside as he was busy working and talking on the phone with a client. The son continued to get his dad's attention but each time the father would grow more tired and irritated of his son's actions.

Finally, the father gets off the phone and the son runs up to his dad and says, "dad, what do you do for work?"

The father says, "I'm a project manager for a financial corporation."

The next question from the young son was, "dad, how much do you make an hour?"

At that moment, the father was furious and thought for some reason that this question was totally disrespectful and out of line. The father answered, "That's none of your business son now go to your room!"

Sadly the son went up the stairs to his room. The father had taken this time to cool down and try to figure out what his son was trying to get at with all the questions.

Fifteen minutes later, the father goes up to his son's room to check up on him. The son is sitting there on his bed moping and the father asks his son a question. "Son, tell me why you asked me what I made per hour?"

The son looked up and smiled and said, "Because I wanted to pay you for an hour so that you could have lunch with me."

The son just wanted his father to be present. He wanted his dad to give some quality time and undivided attention to him. Sure, you're available; you're home with him which is more than a lot of other fathers can say. But what good is it if he feels that you don't even "see" him. He may as well be home alone.

As fathers, our lives can be hectic with family, work and everything else in between. I should know, I'm guilty of this myself at times. We as fathers need to realize that we cannot buy our children's love and affection. At the end of the day, they just want our time. They want to be the focus of our attention and know that we actually care about their lives and what's going on in their own little world. This is also true as they grow up. Time with you will always be the most important thing to them. Can you imagine your dad being there but "not" being there? Imagine playing in your basketball or soccer games and looking for your dad in the crowd but he isn't there because he always has some excuse not to be there. Or even worse, your dad is there at the games but he's constantly on the phone or texting someone else. Of course, mom is there but dad…..not so much.

Do you remember that sinking feeling? After a while you became numb to it but it still affected you. Believe it or not, there are men out there that live by this theory of being in the home but mentally somewhere else. You should think more of yourself than a roof of someone's head and some clothes and food in your child's stomach. Push comes to shove, DFACS can provide that for your child! You have the ability to shape a child's future by how you live, the lessons you teach and the love that you show towards them. They only want your time and they grow up so fast...make it count!

These are our future senators, presidents, CEOs, military personnel, librarians and teachers. We can't just ignore them and hope that they grow up with the morals and values that we want them to have.

QUICK FATHER TIPS

- Be present AND available. There are seven days in the week and **SOMEDAY** ain't one of them!

- Time waits for no man but it sure flies by you're a kid! Get involved now, before both pass you by.

A PRESENT FATHER

A present father takes the time to KNOW their child. They ask them questions and pick their little brains to see what's going on in the inside. Fathers should know certain patterns and ways about their children. They should know their child's personality, behavior, attitudes, etc. Being present is knowing when something isn't right with your child just by the way they answered you or by a particular facial gesture that they make. Being a present father is knowing that you've laid the foundation so that when there's a problem or a challenge for the child, they know they can come to you and talk to you about it. There's no greater feeling than having your child come to you saying, "dad, I gotta problem…..can I talk to you about it?"

These are some of the moments we should live for. And it's only in moments like these that it will either make you or break you because they could end up being some very teachable moments. What am I saying? If you shut that child down during their most vulnerable moments by saying something like, "Is that all it is?? That's not a real problem!! Go do some homework or something!" This will crush a child and they will pretty much never open up to you again. It may not have been a big deal to you, but it was definitely a huge concern for them. We have to let them know that their feelings are important and that they matter too.

Now, on the flipside of things, if you listen to the child and respond in kind, you are golden! Children crave attention and genuine feedback. It re-assures them that you are there for them and that they matter. For example, when your child approaches you with an issue that's important to them, take the time to listen and help to enlighten the young one. When they feel that you do care about what matters to them, they are much more apt to come to you more and take to heart what you have to say. You have now created a bridge of trust and have kept the communication lines open!

Merely being "available" just doesn't cut it with children, it just doesn't. You, as the father end up losing out in the long run due to the fact that you are missing out on some of the most defining moments in a child's life. I know a young lady (we'll call her Sue for the sake of the story) who grew up with a father and mother in the home. The way she describes her father growing up, he was "available" but not "present" for her. It really bothered her growing up even to this day as an adult because she felt like her dad should have been "present" in a lot of moments in her life. He would hardly come to see her cheer at football games always saying that he had something else that he needed to do. When Sue performed in plays at the school and at the church, the results often end up the same. This repeated activity over time took a toll on her and her relationship with her dad (not to mention she was a daddy's girl). This story is going somewhere just stay with me.

She eventually grew up, got married and some years later they had their first child together. It was a beautiful time but things started changing as she was insistent with her husband about him being equally involved in the baby's everyday life (feeding the baby, changing it, burping it, etc.). After a while the husband finally sat his wife down and told her plainly, "look, I'm not your dad so stop treating me like I'm him!" He continued on by saying, "I love my child just as much as you do so please stop putting me in the same category as your dad. You have no right to compare me to him in my actions with my child."

She quickly got the message and they were able to make things work but did you see what happened right there? Because of her relationship or lack thereof with her father who was "available" but not "present", she went back to that place in time when she had her child and she started looking at her husband in the same manner in which her dad was acting towards her. If you get nothing else out of this, please understand that quality time with your child is priceless and will mean the world to them mentally and spiritually.

Be "Present" AND "Available".

There was a time when I was in college and I had come home for the Christmas holidays on winter break. I got a chance to meet with some of my high school buddies for a couple of drinks at a restaurant. We started talking about school, life and then family. Now, growing up, I was always picked on by these same buddies of mine for being in the church all of the time. There was choir rehearsal, usher board meetings, youth empowerment camp, etc. They would even tease me and call me "choir boy" (for obvious reasons). It bothered me somewhat but never to the point where I was severely depressed or just didn't want to go to church anymore. I say all of this to say that my parents both were very clear about our faith and our family.

My dad said that you get out of them what you put into them. Anyway, the guys and I are at the restaurant and we're laughing about all of this now but then they said some things to me that really shocked me. One of my buddies lay claim that he wished his dad was around for him like my dad was for me. He admired the fact that my dad stayed on me and my siblings and provided structure for us. He said that yeah he was able to do what he wanted growing up because his mom always had to work so he was alone a lot of the times but he would have much rather been with his dad. He also said that this is why he would come over to my house all the time. It was the closest that he ever came to at having a dad. My dad would talk to this guy and ask him questions about school and what he wanted to do in life. It made a big impact on him. I was floored! My other buddy pretty much echoed the same thing. He stated that he actually enjoyed coming over to my house and helping me clean my room and the basement.

Now by this time I'm looking at them like I see two aliens! WHAT??? Seriously!!!! He said that when he was there he really felt like he was family because my dad would treat him as such. My point here men is that we are so powerful as fathers and positive male figures but we don't tap into that and make ourselves accountable. These men that I just spoke about realized early in life how "present" and "available" my dad was to me and my siblings. We HAVE to keep ourselves and each other accountable for the children that lack fathers and positive male figures. By the way, these two grown men now STILL call my father from time to time to check in on him and reminisce every once in a while.

QUICK FATHER TIPS

- The most precious and valuable thing you could ever give your child is T-I-M-E!!
- Kids know when you're not present and available....so make sure that you are.
- If you can't give them the attention and time they need, somebody else will, and not the right kind either
- When you're with your child, listening to them gives them a world of confidence.

FATHERS AND SONS

Now this is a bond that, if done correctly, will last a lifetime. Now I know there are quite a few fathers out there that have only girls (I happen to be one of those blessed fathers) but I'm also a son so I know how proud my dad was to get two boys so that his name could be passed down. Not only will the name be passed on, but other traditions and heirlooms that a father would pass down to his son(s). The thing with fathers and sons is that, as a father, you want your son to be like you a little bit but at the same time you want him to be his own man as well. In some instances, it's like watching yourself grow up right in front of your very own eyes!

This bond is so imperative because, as a young boy this is where you learn integrity, character and how to carry yourself as an upright, respectful human being. It's also a challenging time during the teen years and early 20's because this is when the young man starts to come into his own with his own ideas, opinions and views of the world and of himself. At the same time, the father will soon learn that there will come a time when he actually has to stop being the father (the over seer, protector, disciplinarian, etc.) and start to become an advisor to his son.

This relationship was crucial to me as a son because this is also how I learned so many things about being a responsible young man. I grew up learning from my father about character, hard work, and understanding the importance of being dependable and keeping my word to others. I also learned about respect, being a good friend and respecting females. As I became older, my father game me more leeway and allowed me to make decisions and encounter situations without intervening. He was always there to coach and advise me on things that I may have missed in my thinking process. I'm sure this wasn't easy for him to do but he had to do it.

Part of his teachings was for me to learn some things from my own experiences. The best part about it was that, if it was a really major or intense situation, I could count on him to go back into "dad mode" if necessary. My father and I shared a love for the sport of football and we connected a great deal in that aspect as well.

One of the most important lessons I learned from my father was how to love a woman and become a man that understood what it means to properly love and respect them. He showed me how to treat women by watching him interact with my mom. Now he isn't the flowers and candy type of guy but he loves my mom dearly and it shows. He would hug her and kiss her from time to time and my brother and I would just gag when we were younger because we thought it was disgusting! He would have conversations with her and take her out sometimes. There would be times that she would be cooking and he would walk up behind her and hug her and then pop her one time on her butt. I find myself doing that with my wife now! My father educated me and my brother on women and taught us to give them the utmost respect and to never lay a hand on them. He went on to say that they these women we will encounter are someone's daughters and sisters. He lives what he instilled in us. These are just some of the things that my dad taught me along the way.

My dad wasn't much of a talker when I was growing up but he was always there for us. He NEVER missed a football game. He would take me and my brother in the yard and toss the ball with us and show us some of his moves. I could go on but I want to bring the message home to fathers out there that they matter and that they are so important to a young boy's life. Mothers can teach the young boys how to love women, be polite and respectful and things like that. The biggest challenge for single moms is trying to raise a boy to be a man.

Fathers are really needed in the involvement of raising these young men because our future partially depends on them. We have generations of young men lost out there in the streets just wondering aimlessly and not knowing what's going to happen to them from one day to the next. The enemy is rapidly destroying our young men and if we don't take them back from the enemy (i.e. the streets, drugs, gangs, etc.) our future looks very dismal. One of the biggest reasons fathers are so needed by their sons is the fact of validation.

Every son wants to eventually go out into the world and make something of himself. Do you know why that is? Deep down inside he wants to be validated by his father. A son just wants that smile on his dad's face and to hear him say, "Son, well done. I've very proud of you." To be able to hear that from your father along with an "I love you son", that makes all the difference in the entire world. Mission accomplished! It's no different than our Heavenly Father saying "well done My good and faithful servant, well done!"

Now, I will admit that the "I love you" for a lot of fathers is hard to say. Nonetheless, it is very important that you clearly communicate your feelings to your son.

Young men should never have to learn how to be a man on the streets. No man should leave his son or sons with their mom and hope that they will learn how to be men on their own. No young man should ever have to go through that. Unfortunately, they do every day and then the world wonders why some of these men, if not most, have self-esteem issues, anger and relationship issues. One of the worst feelings in the world is being that child who's always wondering why their dad left or even never was around in the first place. Guilt sets in at first for a while and then anger and resentment kicks in later. Some men are able to channel those emotions into something they are good at and end up succeeding and excelling in the career of their choice. Others hold on to that bitterness that allows them to grow cold hearted and numb to feelings.

Fathers should want to be in their son's lives so that they can pass down invaluable information and family possessions and materials to their son. One bad lesson learned on the streets and he could die at a moment's notice. We have generations of young boys who are lost today walking aimlessly up and down the streets of America. They don't know who they are half of the time and they certainly don't know WHO'S they are!! We need to invest time into our young men or else the streets will.

If you are a father that hasn't connected with his son, don't use time or money as an excuse. There are only 24 hours in a day and that has never changed nor will it ever. If the mother is making it difficult so what! Your son probably doesn't know that and is wondering why you won't make the effort to come see him. He's wondering why he isn't worth the fight with his mom to see him. He'll wonder is he even worth it to you. Well is he? Is your son worth the fight, the extra effort to establishing a relationship with him?

QUICK FATHER TIPS

- Use your life as a teachable lesson to your son
- Listen to your son to understand.......not just to respond.
- Your son is your prince; a king in training ....lead him and teach him as such.
- Teach him to respect all women and why it's important to do so.
- They will make mistakes; make sure they know that you will always be there for them, no matter what!

FATHERS AND DAUGHTERS

Now this is a topic that I know all too well. Being that I'm a father of three beautiful girls, I know first-hand the importance and significance of a father's role in the lives of little girls. Girls are SOOO different than boys but at the same time, they are the biggest protectors of their fathers! As females, they are nurturers by nature but what they should also learn is the proper way love is to be given to them by men. Girls know how to love (for the most part) but understanding how to receive it from young men is crucial to how they get in and establish relationships with guys.

It's so vital that they get this understanding from us because, if not, they will learn it through media, ill-advised friends and others who just want to take advantage of them. We as men are looked upon naturally as strong protectors and providers (in a sense). Little girls who have their fathers in their lives think the world of them. They believe that their father is "DA MAN!" They believe he can do no wrong. The daughters get their self-esteem, their self-worth, their validation from their father. When that is done correctly, these knuckle-headed boys better watch out because now they are dealing with a young lady who knows she is loved, she is beautiful and that she doesn't have to settle for anything less than what she's willing to accept. That's a young lady who has been properly equipped by her father.

Young girls are very observant and impressionable, so when they see the interaction between their mother and father, they take that as how love and relationships are supposed to be. Even if you aren't with the mother, you still can show your little angel how women are to receive love from a man with your current girlfriend or wife. You can also show her how men treat women by how you interact with their mother or other women. Girls get a heavy dosage of relationship lessons from their parents and this affects them well into adulthood. For example, if she sees her father abusing her mother physically and/or mentally over the years, she's thinking that this is how it is. Another example could be when there is no father around and the young girl is taught (either by media, movies or friends) that love is sex. Therefore, she's sleeping around with guys because she thinks that's the only time she can get their full attention and love.

Our young girls are being exploited and sought out by sick predators that lurk in the background and feed on young, innocent and low self-esteemed girls who haven't been loved properly by a father or positive male figure. It is so much harder to trick a young girl when she knows her worth and knows who she is. I tell my girls all of the time that daddy loves each and every one of them. They know that they are all my princesses! I tell them that they are beautiful and that they are capable of doing anything they set their minds to. I reinforce that with them every day until it takes root in them and they believe it themselves. We, as fathers, are leaders. We set standards and our children watch us closely. The standards that we set are the ones they take with them for life.

One day, as I was picking up my girls from afterschool care, my oldest daughter hopped in the car and began telling me about her day.

She said, "daddy, this boy wanted to borrow a pencil from me and I told him no."

She went on to say, "Then he gets mad at me and told me I was ugly! I looked at him and I said no I'm not, I'm beautiful because my daddy tells me every day!"

It took everything in my power not to laugh but I was so proud of the fact that she didn't cave in and start thinking, "am I ugly?" She said it with such conviction because she finally believed it herself. Her father just validated her! I was so proud of my baby girl. I had a tear or two that I had to fight back because I started thinking that she's got it now. She won't be easily swayed by the comments of others. She didn't need outside validation because she gets it regularly from her father.

I've been told by multiple men and women (older than me) when they find out that I have three girls that I'm a blessed man. They say that girls take care of their fathers when they get older (we'll see lol!). I honestly feel like I'm blessed regardless because I was given this awesome opportunity and esteemed honor to be a father to three wonderful little girls. Our girls need us more than ever because they are growing up in the age of technology where sexual exploitation is exposed to them at such an early age now. They need their fathers to help process some of the information they are receiving. The correct understanding of love and how it's to be received from a man is almost as important as breathing. Honestly, our sons and daughters need the correct understanding which is why fathers, again, play such a profound part in the growth and stability of children.

If you don't have a relationship with your daughter(s) I admonish you to do so as soon as you can. It's an unspeakable and indescribable feeling that is just overwhelmingly joyous. It's a high that you never really come down from! I love my girls and I learn so much from them on a daily basis. One thing is certain, they love their father! Girls that have a great relationship with their dad have a certain loyalty to them that is like no other. As a matter of fact, it's almost scary.

I can recall one instance where my dad had my sister in the car with him and he was racing to get home for some reason or another. Half way home he gets pulled over by a police officer. My sister is probably 7 or 8 years old at the time of this incident and she's asking my dad why the police stopped them. He told her that he didn't know but to just sit back and be quiet. My sister is really feisty and never took too well to someone messing with our father. The officer soon approaches the vehicle and asks my father for his license and registration.

My sister belts out to my father, "you don't need to show'em your license, he needs to show you his identification!" Now if my father could have melted in his seat, I think he would have. He somehow kept it together and produced the information requested of him. Thankfully, the officer thought that it was very cute for the daughter to take up for her father.

When you have a great relationship with your daughter, they actually turn into the protectors and sometimes the providers as well. It's really the same way with mothers and their sons. I've also noticed with my girls that there is constant competition for my attention and affection. It's a never ending battle to have their father to themselves. I work really hard (and so should you) on making sure that each one gets individual time with me so that they can talk about things that matter to them. They get the one-on-one with me which creates a bond that will last forever.

As they grow older and start dating, I do know that they will value heavily what you think about their love interest once they become serious with them. Girls tend to look for values and traits of their fathers in the men they become attracted to and date. They also look to find guys that treat them like their fathers do (from a love and respect aspect). Please remember that if we don't teach them someone else will. These are our princesses and we want to make sure as best we can that when the time comes for her to take a husband, he will love and treat her with just as much love and respect as we do.

QUICK FATHER TIPS

- Your daughter(s) are your princesses; your queens in training……..lead them and teach them as such.
- Listen to your daughters and just be there for them. They don't always need us to "fix" everything. Sometimes they want us to listen and be a sounding board for them.
- Whatever they tell you, don't fly off the handle! Yes, it will be hard sometimes, but if you do you will lose them. Listen and console and do your best to advise.
- Make sure they understand that whatever the situation is, you will be there for them.

EXCUSES ARE FOR THE WEAK!

If it's one thing I can't stand it's a man who gives every excuse in the book for not being a part of their child or children's lives. I think it's selfish and shows insecurity of their manhood. I've heard a ton of excuses for not being involved in their kid's lives. The one thing that gets me is that not at one point in time did they ever think about how their kids would feel when dad isn't there for their first ballgame or dance recital. They never think about the child and the pain they go through when other kids talk about their dad's and what they did with them the past weekend and the fun that they had. These fathers just think about themselves and have a pity party because they aren't where they want to be in life or where they feel they need to be.

Life beats EVERYONE down from time to time but it's up to us to determine how we respond and get back up. If you are a father of a child you must understand that the child didn't ask to be here. If you were not ready to have or father a child, you shouldn't have been doing what it takes to make a child! It is all too popular among the male species to go out when you're a young man and "sew your wild oats". Young men are taught this but they aren't taught that if you end up impregnating a woman, you need to step up and make sure that you take care of your child and establish a great relationship with them. We, as men, are taught to hunt or chase women for sexual pleasures but there are not enough of us teaching about how to properly court a woman and it not be for sexual gain.

There are so many broken homes because of the improper way young men are taught to attract a female. No one ever teaches us how to KEEP her! Yeah, we do whatever it takes to attract her and make her like us or want us. After a while, the woman tends to want more and now we're stuck. We're stuck because we've never been taught how to stay in a relationship. We don't know intimacy or affection, so all of that is new and awkward to us. Since this is the root of a lot of relationship issues, it trickles down into the relationship with our children. Enough of this for now…let's stay focused on the children!

Some of you don't have the relationship that you would like to have with your child because you say that the mother is bitter or hateful towards you. Do you think it could have been because you deceived her in some way? Maybe you made her believe that you all were exclusive when you really weren't. It could be a number of things but this is something that as a father you will have to deal with and find a way to resolve.

Gentlemen, listen closely, you are what the mothers tell the children you are until you prove her wrong with your actions towards your children. The bottom line is establishing the connection that your child needs. Regardless of the way the mother sees you, it is your duty and mission in life to show her and your child that you need to be in your child's life…period. If you have friends telling you it ain't worth it and to just move on, you need to immediately acquire some new friends.

I have one example where there was a young man named Jason that claimed he wanted to see his daughters but the mother (Martha) wouldn't let him. Apparently Martha was upset because he decided to move on and no longer wanted to be in a relationship with her. She doesn't take the message too well and threatens to keep Jason's girls away from him so that he can never see them. I told him that this can only happen if he allows it. He mentioned that he thought about getting a lawyer to see what his rights are and what he can do but lost interest because he felt it took too much money. Hello?? Too much money? How much is too much when it comes to the relationship with your children? I just couldn't understand his logic. To me, he basically just put a price tag on his efforts to try and establish a relationship with his daughters.

REALLY????
I asked Jason if he had tried to sit down and talk to the Martha rationally and he said that he did but it was unsuccessful. She wasn't happy and she didn't want him to be happy. It's one of those things where she wanted him to hurt like she did. That was her way of making that happen. I strongly encouraged him try different ways and avenues to create consistent contact with his girls but he claimed that he was just tired of trying.

Wow.........tired of trying to be there for your flesh and blood because the mother is reportedly being difficult? Thank God I've never been in that situation but I believe with everything in my being that I would exhaust all of my resources and time and talent into getting my relationship with my kids again. I just couldn't bear the thought that my child is on the other side wondering if their dad even cares about them.

As a man, we should all get to a point in life where excuses are no more. Accountability should be in everything and all that we do. See, being a father you may have to cut yourself away from some of your friends because they won't understand what you need to do as a father. The young man who I just spoke about didn't want to go the extra mile to do what it took to ensure that he could see his girls. He allowed the mother to dictate his relationship with his girls. Needless to say his girls didn't care for him that much. They thought he didn't want to be bothered with them. When he was finally able to communicate with his girls it took years for them to get to a place where they could have a good relationship. Don't be that guy.

There are not enough apologies in the world that could soothe the hurt that the child endured because their father didn't want to go the extra mile or two....or three to reconnect with them. This has a lasting effect on the child emotionally, mentally, spiritually and relationally. These fathers don't sit and think about the magnitude of their actions or lack thereof. This is a selfish and cowardly act on the part of the father.

It's so funny how we don't accept excuses for our paychecks being late from our job. Nor do we accept bad customer service because we're using our hard earned money to pay for the service and/or the product. We also don't accept people disrespecting us or trying to belittle us. But when it comes to trying to create a relationship with your child, the excuses become all too common. A lot of times our priorities are out of whack and that's really sad. What's even worse is that those people in your circle don't even check you on it. One thing's for sure.........misery loves company.

QUICK FATHER TIPS

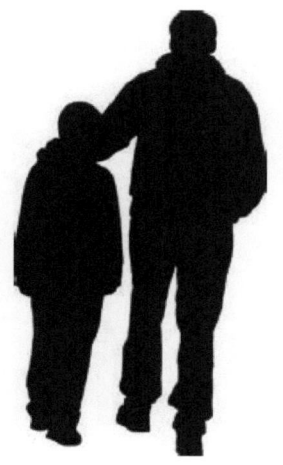

- Excuses show your incompetence for making something happen.
- Cop outs only lead to more cop outs.
- When you stop placing the blame on others and take full responsibility, progress can begin.

YOUR SEED = A NATION

This portion of the book is for ALL men regardless of the relationship with your child(ren). I don't think we understand how powerful our seed is, not only to ourselves and our family, but to the world. You may think I'm stretching this thing but just keep reading. Maybe I can open your eyes and enlighten you on a thing or two about your worth and your legacy.

You see, every time you "plant a seed" (i.e. impregnate a woman) you set off a chain reaction called the miracle of life. This seed is fertilized and nurtured by the female egg thus giving way to the miracle of a beautiful baby. Children are a gift from God and an extension of you and your past. The legacy is created when the man and woman are together and from that union generations will form and grow and expand. Your child is a reflection of you and your heritage. After you are gone your child or children are the evidence that you existed. They are the fingerprints of the past generations and of you.

On the other hand, when you plant seeds in several women and you don't stay with any of them, this results in several "broken" nations. I say broken because they don't have the cornerstones that they need to lay their solid foundation upon. Our society is filled with "broken nations" and we need to fix this. The best way to fix this is to STOP sleeping around with every woman until you can find the one suitable to nurture and carry your seed. Some men plant their seeds in anything that will lie down with them! It is crucial that we become more protective of our seed because it is our legacy and future generations are at stake. We need to make better choices with the women we choose. The type of woman you lay with determines in part how your legacy and future generations will turn out. Your seed = generations.

For example, look at Abraham from the Bible. God promised him that his descendants would ultimately comprise many nations. Many nations! The name Abraham itself means "father of a multitude". God also promised him that kings would descend from the aged patriarch!

Now imagine for a second, through you, that child could become the next president of the United States of America, the next Einstein or Oprah! What I'm saying is your seed is special and powerful and is potentially world-changing. Wouldn't you want a woman that you can love and respect and receive the same in return? You are a King and you need to be in search of a queen and not just trying to "scratch an itch".

Now I know all men don't have the wrong motive. There are some situations where you both were in love and in a great relationship at one time but for whatever reason moved on. My desire is that the young men who are out there "having fun" would sit back and take another look at how you "have fun". Bringing a child into this world is a serious matter and one that should be taken as such. If you aren't ready to take on that responsibility, find other ways to have your fun and live life. Kids don't ask to be here and just because you aren't ready to be a father doesn't mean that this child is just gonna go away.

Chris was a guy I knew that loved to play the field and he had about 4 kids each with a different lady. He saw his kids when he could but never on a consistent basis. He was never around when any of the kids needed him (emotionally, physically, etc.) but when he did come around he would always have on the latest fashions but could never seem to have any money OR OTHER SUPPORT of any kind for his children. I could go on but you get the point about Chris. His children represent the "broken nations" mentioned in this section. When I say broken nations I'm referring to the parental foundation that his children lacked. Of course they had their mothers but they didn't have their father. Remember, earlier in the book I spoke about a child needing BALANCE in their lives. The children here didn't have the balance and they had an emptiness or a void in their hearts where their dad is supposed to be. This lack of balance effects self-esteem, happiness, confidence, emotional stability, future problems with potential relationships, etc.

I know that this section of the book may offend some men. It's understandable but at least now you may become "awakened" and take a second look on how you "spread your seed". When children don't come from a stable environment chances are that they are more likely to act out at home and at school. Due to displaced feelings and emotions, they don't know what to do with them let alone know how to process them. These kids can grow up and have careers and be successful but when it comes to their personal growth, feelings and relationships, they will most likely struggle quite a bit in those areas.

QUICK FATHER TIPS

- Teach your son the importance of his "scepter" and how it shouldn't be thrown around to just any woman that will have him.
- Understand that the legacy you leave behind is due to the choices that you made in choosing a woman.
- Know that your "seed" is your prized possession and you should treat it as such.

BE RELATABLE

Gentlemen, please be a father that's relatable. The worst thing that you can do is be a father that is quick to bark at and criticize your children for the wrong they've done and pretend as though you've never done it. After a while you subconsciously create this persona about you that you are or were perfect at one time. One thing that I've noticed with my children, and also what I wanted from my dad, was to hear about his flaws and mistakes. They want to know I'm not perfect either. When we sit down to have a dialogue with our children and we reveal our setbacks, failures and mistakes, that allows our children to see another side of us. The human side. It's a great way to connect with your children in order to drive home a message that you really want them to understand.

I'll never forget the time when my 7 year old was in the store with me and I was buying some grocery for dinner that night, she really wanted some candy and I said no and that she couldn't have any. Well, she took it upon herself to grab it anyway because she wanted it. After I completed my transaction with the cashier, my girls and I were walking out of the store. Half way to the exit I noticed my 7 year old was behind me walking with her jacket on, humped over. So now I'm thinking, "what is wrong with my child?" You see the picture! So I ask her what's wrong. She says nothing is wrong but she won't stand up straight. Right then I knew something wasn't right so I asked her to stand up straight and when she did...............well out came the candy. I was livid!

At that moment all I saw was red because I was so angry and disappointed with her. I grabbed the candy and we marched back to the cashier to take the candy back. I gave her a tongue lashing and made her apologize to the cashier and manager of the store.

When we got to the car I explained the severity of doing something like that. I won't say what else happened to her but let's just say that she didn't really have a good day that day. Later that evening, I was on the phone with my mother and I was talking to her about the situation and how I handled it. My heart was really heavy that night because I had to discipline my daughter and explain that her penalty had to match the action that she took. My mother laughed on the phone and told me a story about me actually doing the same thing when I was my daughter's age. She told me how she handled it. The timing of that conversation couldn't have been more perfect. The next morning when my 7 year old awoke, I gave her a big hug and told her that I loved her dearly. I asked her to have a seat next to me on the steps. I explained to her how when I was about her age that there was this G.I. Joe action figure that I wanted so bad but my mom said no. I felt the same way that my daughter did and I took it. I told my daughter what happened to me when my mom caught me with the toy (I can't say but nowadays they would call it child abuse! LOL!). The important thing is that my story stuck with my 7 year old. She's now showing her younger sister what to do and what not to do and why.

Stories about your misfortunes help your children more than you'll ever know. Don't be afraid to share with your child your mistakes. It's better they learn from you so that you can help them either correct or avoid pitfalls. It's only when we pretend to have always had wisdom, that we unknowingly cause a disconnect between us and our child. The key is to not only communicate with your child, but to connect with them.

QUICK FATHER TIPS

- Your life experiences = invaluable nuggets of knowledge for your child(ren).
- Get off of your soapbox and connect with your child through mistakes
- You can be relatable without having to be their friend.

DON'T DISAPPOINT

I can't begin to tell you how many times I've heard young men and women talk about their fathers who were never around. Growing up, my buddy Scott would get so excited when his dad would call him during the week and say, "hey big guy! I'm coming to pick you up this weekend so that we can have some guy time and get some ice cream!" Scott would just walk around all that week beaming like the sun and happy as could be because his dad was coming to pick him up on Friday after school. Well, Friday came around and I would sit with Scott and we would talk about our favorite cartoons, movies, heroes, etc. As we talked and talked, time slowly drifted away and evening was soon upon us. I could tell he was getting a little worried about his dad not showing up. I told him that maybe he should call and check on him. Scott got up and went inside to call his dad. He was able to reach him and found out that his dad was still at work. His dad told him that he would be a little late but that he would be there and not to worry. Scott started beaming again as he hung up the phone. He came back outside to the steps where I was and told me what his dad said. With all being well in the world at least thus far, we continued to chat about TV shows and the like. It wasn't too much later that Scott's mother called him in the house for a minute. She needed to tell him something.

Scott came back outside a little later and he was so hurt. His dad wasn't coming after all. It was 9:45PM and his mom had been trying to reach his dad for a while and he wasn't returning the calls. I felt so bad for him. I asked him if he wanted me to hang with him for a while but he softly declined trying desperately to hold back the tears and disappointment in his dad. I felt so bad that I was even angry at his dad. We said our good byes and I went home feeling really bad for my friend. I asked my dad "how could a man do that to his own kid?"

My father just looked at me and shook his head, "I don't know son, maybe we can all go out tomorrow and get some ice cream and help him take his mind off of it for a while."

"I like that idea dad!" I said.

Gentlemen, if you are at the point where you can come visit and pick up your child please do so. **Do what you say you are going to do**, especially when it comes to your child. In case you don't know, it's a devastating feeling to your child when you don't deliver when you say you are going to. The sad part for the fathers is that the children don't forget. You can do one hundred things right after that but they will never forget how you left them hanging. Kids don't really get into the money and gifts and material goods that a lot of fathers try to throw at their children when they can't be there. They just want your TIME! Unfortunately, fathers will spend insane amounts of money and buy priceless gifts to show they are sorry but it only lasts for a while. Memories with your child are things that you can't buy and last a lifetime. The funny thing is…..kids know this but fathers don't………..until it's too late.

The sad thing is that these kids who grow up with this disappointment from their fathers time and time again, end up having relationship problems. They also will have a hard time making friends because they don't want to run the risk of that person not coming around anymore. These children usually harbor those feelings of anger, abandonment and disappointment for a long, long time (again, broken nations). This is quite some heavy baggage and even if they are fortunate enough to find someone to love and eventually marry, that person is going to have to be a very special and patient person in order to deal with their mate's heavy burdens. This is all because you didn't have the time to sew into your child's life because something or someone was more important to you than they are. ARE YOU SERIOUS!!!!

You actually have some asinine fathers that think that their kids didn't want to see them anyway because they were a failure to them. How would you know that if you didn't take time to spend with them? It's interesting how these fathers love to put words in the mouths of the children they helped produce but never see! Who does this??? It's an utterly and complete cop out in the worst and most pathetic way. Don't speak for the child.......let them speak for themselves! Trust me, I understand that things don't always work out in a relationship but, for God's sake, please don't penalize the child.

You may be in a position where you aren't where you want to be in life and maybe you aren't making
the money you feel you should be making but guess what.........your child DOES NOT CARE! All

they want is you and your time. Nothing can make a child feel more secure than to have fun and spend quality time with their father. For some reason, fathers can't seem to understand this simple concept. You know what.....I take that back........I know exactly what it is! It's that good ole' fashion male pride/ego. This is also the same pride/ego that gets us into a lot of trouble and situations that we have a hard time getting out of (if we can).
Gentlemen, we have to do better. Our children deserve better than what we're giving them. They are our future and we need them to be ready to take on the world and whatever it has in store for them. We can't have them trying to solve world issues and working on world crisis when in the back of their minds they are still having "daddy" issues. This thing is real and we as men need to step back into the lives of our children and start planting another seed. Not the baby kind! This seed will be to reinforce our love, support, guidance and stability so that they will have the balance that they need to be successful in their lives, not professionally but in their relationships with their friends and loved ones. As fathers, one of our main objectives should be building foundations for the future.

Many of us are too busy worrying only about ourselves and what we can gain and accomplish. Little do we know that our lives are not to be lived for ourselves but for others. We should live to love and serve not love and acquire. Life is bigger than us and we have to realize this in order to be better fathers. Let's stop disappointing our children and each other and start making strides to right the wrongs that we've done for so long.

It's easy to continue to keep going down the wrong path because it's familiar and comfortable. Things will only change when we do. Fathers are the key to a better and brighter future for our children and our world.

QUICK FATHER TIPS

- I think we're good here ☺.

CONCLUSION

This book wasn't written to hit men over the head. It's more of a "reality check" to get us back where we need to be with our children. Our children need us regardless of what the mother says, what the media says and what society says. If you were brave enough to read this book to the end, no longer are you able to use any excuses if you are not in good standing with your child(ren). No longer are you able to hide behind your lies and layers of empty excuses. You will now be held fully accountable for how you interact with your children because if you didn't know then, now you know better. When you know better you are supposed to do better. You should not want to be known for your scholastic or professional achievements alone. Instead, your proudest and highest achievement should be from your child when they say, "I have the best dad in the world!"

> Now, that right there my friends,
> trumps everything!

Other Writings by
 Chad D. Bumgarner

CHAD'S PLAYBOOK TO EFFECTIVE LEADERSHIP

The book is meant to take mediocre or good leaders and turn them into better, more effective leaders.

2015©
ISBN 9-780692-519349

For more info. contact Chad Bumgarner @
info@chadbumgarner.co
www.chadbumgarner.co
twitter: @chad_bumgarner

Chad D. Bumgarner
www.Chadbumgarner.co

www.ingramcontent.com/pod-product-compliance
Lightning Source LLC
Chambersburg PA
CBHW042126080426
42734CB00001B/12